THE STORY OF THE SECOND WORLD WAR

Paul Dowswell

Designed by Tom Lalonde, Sam Barrett & Will Dawes

Illustrated by Ian McNee

Edited by Jane Chisholm   Managing designer: Stephen Moncrieff

Consultant: Terry Charman, Imperial War Museum

Contents

A British Lancaster bomber
photographed during a raid on the
city of Hamburg, in northern Germany

HMS *Campbeltown* at St. Nazaire, during a British commando raid on Nazi-occupied France in March 1942, painted by Norman Wilkinson

The world at war

The Second World War was the greatest conflict in history. Even set against the carnage of the First World War, it was the most catastrophic event of the 20th century. At least 50 million people were killed, and lives were shattered on a scale that can scarcely be imagined. Even today, the shadow of the War still fuels the tensions, crises and tragedies of international politics.

A map of the War

The Second World War was fought between two opposing alliances, known as the Allies and the Axis Powers, and almost every part of the world was drawn into the conflict.

CANADA

Pacific Ocean

UNITED STATES

Washington

Atlantic Ocean

Pearl Harbor, 1941

NORWAY

FINLAND

Leningrad, 1941-44

SOVIET UNION

SWEDEN

Moscow

Kursk, 1943

DENMARK

BALTIC STATES

IRELAND

GREAT BRITAIN

Battle of Britain, 1940

London

HOLLAND

UKRAINE

BELGIUM

GERMANY

POLAND

Normandy Landings, 1944

FRANCE

SWITZERLAND

SLOVAKIA

HUNGARY

ROMANIA

YUGOSLAVIA

PORTUGAL

SPAIN

ITALY

Rome

ALBANIA

BULGARIA

TURKEY

GREECE

MOROCCO

ALGERIA

El Alamein, 1942

EGYPT

The three Axis nations, Germany, Japan and Italy, reached the height of their power in the summer of 1942. The territory under their control is shown here in red.

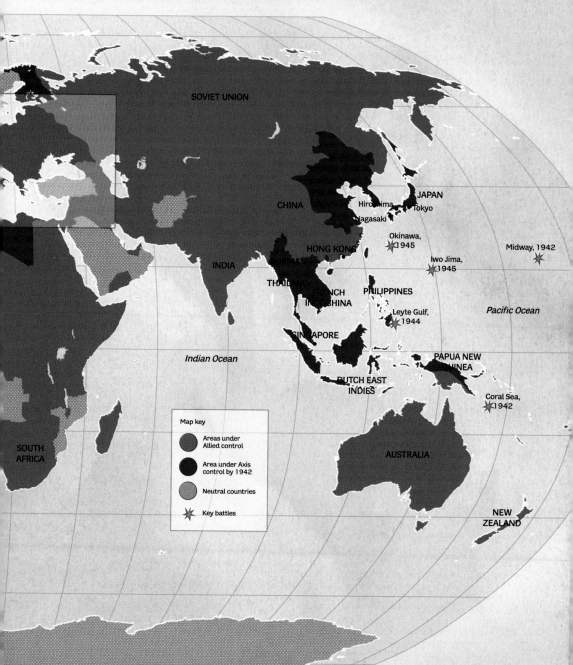

SOVIET UNION

CHINA

Hiroshima
Tokyo
JAPAN
Nagasaki

Okinawa,
1945

Midway, 1942

INDIA

HONG KONG

Iwo Jima,
1945

BURMA
THAILAND
FRENCH
INDOCHINA
PHILIPPINES

Pacific Ocean

Leyte Gulf,
1944

SINGAPORE

Indian Ocean

PAPUA NEW
GUINEA

DUTCH EAST
INDIES

Coral Sea,
1942

Map key

Areas under
Allied control

Area under Axis
control by 1942

Neutral countries

Key battles

SOUTH
AFRICA

AUSTRALIA

NEW
ZEALAND

Berlin University students burn 'forbidden' books, shortly after the Nazis come to power in 1933.

Chapter 1

Building a bonfire

At 11am on November 11, 1918, the guns fell silent on the devastated battlefields of Europe. The First World War was over. There were wild street parties in the capitals of the victorious nations, while the defeated struggled with numb disbelief. Over four years, millions had died in the most bitter conflict the world had ever seen. But, while the fighting was over, tensions remained that would provide the sparks that led directly into the next war – so much so that some historians view the two conflicts as one.

The world the War created

The First World War, sometimes known as 'the Great War', had left Europe exhausted. For much of the War, the two sides had been stuck in bitter deadlock, as each threw its military and industrial might into wearing the other down. By the time the fighting ended, the scale of the destruction was so great that even the victors looked like losers.

Coming to terms

In January 1919, representatives from 32 nations gathered in Paris – and Versailles, just outside the city. They hoped to negotiate a peace agreement that would prove the Great War to be the 'war to end all wars', but many of them disagreed about the terms.

Versailles

Leading the talks at Versailles were the heads of the three most powerful nations on the winning side: Britain, France and the United States. The vanquished nations, Germany, Austria-Hungary and the Turkish empire, were not invited.

US President Woodrow Wilson argued for reconciliation between former enemies. But the French, who had suffered so much during the War that almost half of their men between 20 and 35 had been killed or wounded, pushed for a punishing settlement that would 'Make Germany Pay'. Many British people felt the same, so their Prime Minster, David Lloyd George, reluctantly backed the French.

British, French and American officers react with different degrees of interest to the signing of the treaty at Versailles, France.

A flawed peace

In June, German politicians were summoned to Versailles to sign the peace treaty. Many Germans already felt that victory had been snatched from them and that they had been 'stabbed in the back' by their leaders. They bitterly resented the harsh terms of the treaty. Outraged, many took to the streets in protest, but they had no choice but to accept it. On June 28, 1919, the Germans grudgingly signed the Treaty of Versailles.

The War was officially over. But Lloyd George felt uneasy, remarking: "We shall have to do the whole thing again in twenty years time." He was almost exactly right.

The Russian Revolution

In 1917, a political party called the Bolsheviks had overthrown the government in Russia. Led by Vladimir Ilyich Ulyanov, known as Lenin, they made peace with Germany, and murdered their own royal family.

After three years of bloody civil war, they took power, renaming the country the Soviet Union and transforming it into a communist state.

A new breed of tyranny

The 1920s and early 1930s saw the rise of four tyrannical regimes, all of which would play a leading role in the Second World War.

Hitler and Mussolini

In the 1920s, Germany had been brought to its knees by reparations and the collapse of its economy. Adolf Hitler and his Nazi Party swept to power in 1933, blaming Germany's economic woes on Jews and communists. Hitler believed that getting rid of them, and increasing German military strength, would make the country great again, and the lands to the east of Germany should become *Lebensraum* – living space – for German people.

A similar regime took control in Italy from 1922, led by Benito Mussolini and his Fascist Party. They came to power amid widespread fears of a communist revolution.

Der Führer & il Duce

Hitler, known as *der Führer* (German for 'leader'), was a ruthless character, who was given to tantrums. But he was also a mesmerizing public speaker, who saw fanaticism as a virtue.

"We will not capitulate – no, never! We may be destroyed, but if we are, we shall drag a world with us – a world in flames."

Mussolini, known as *il Duce* (Italian for 'leader'), also had a talent for public speaking. He inspired his followers with dramatic talk of building a 'new Roman empire' for Italy.

"Better to be a lion for a day than a sheep for a hundred years."

Mussolini (left) was both a rival and an inspiration to Hitler, but he became a friend and ally. Here they share tea and cakes in 1937.

Stalin: the man of steel

Josef Jughashvili changed his
surname to Stalin, meaning
'man of steel', when he became
a communist revolutionary.
He went on to rival Hitler in
murderous ruthlessness.

Stalin attempted to turn the Soviet
Union from a peasant society into a
modern industrial nation. This meant that when
the Second World War broke out, the Russians were
able to build large numbers of tanks and guns to
defend themselves from the Germans. But bad
planning led to famine, which cost millions of lives.

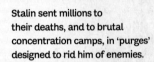

Stalin sent millions to
their deaths, and to brutal
concentration camps, in 'purges'
designed to rid him of enemies.

"Death solves all problems. No man. No problem."

Stalin's solution to political difficulties.

Japan's ruthless generals

Japan had been on the winning side in the First
World War, but had gained little from it. An island
empire with few natural resources, Japan set its
sights on China, and the colonies of Britain, France
and the Netherlands. In the 1930s, the Japanese
government came under the control of a group
of military leaders who decided that war was the
way to world power. They had no single ruler, as in
Germany, Italy or the Soviet Union, but the regime
was just as ruthless, and its army just as cruel.

"...If there are any opponents to the Imperial Way
[meaning Japanese expansion] we shall give them an
injection with a bullet and a bayonet."

General Sadao Araki threatens moderate Japanese politicians.

The Nazi-Soviet Pact

On August 21, 1939, a week
before the Second World
War began, the world was
shocked when Germany and
the Soviet Union signed a
pact promising not to attack
each other.

Politically, the Nazis and the
communists appeared to be
polar opposites, but it was
a friendship of convenience.
Hitler secretly intended to
conquer the Soviet Union,
but he knew he needed more
time to build up his forces.

A satirical cartoon from the
Washington Star depicts the
Nazi-Soviet Pact as a sham
wedding between Hitler (left)
and Stalin.

Between the Wars

Disappointingly, peace didn't bring the rewards the victors of the First World War had expected. Britain and France emerged much weaker, as the fighting had drained their wealth and resources.

The United States, in turn, had become the world's most powerful nation. But many Americans didn't want their country to take part in world affairs. Isolationism – the desire not to be concerned with events in other parts of the world – became a powerful political force.

Unemployed Americans advertise their skills in Chicago, 1934.

Vulnerable empires

Some of Britain and France's overseas colonies came under threat – both from people in the colonies who were beginning to demand independence, and from Germany, Italy and Japan, whose governments were intent on grabbing the colonies for themselves.

In Britain, many people had come to believe Germany had been badly treated at Versailles, and that Hitler should be 'appeased' – given what he wanted, within reason. So when the Germans sent troops into the Rhineland, some claimed he was 'only marching into his own back yard'. The French wanted Hitler to be stopped, but without British support, they had to back down.

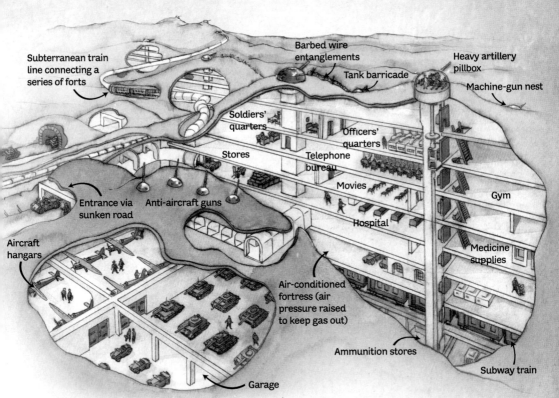

Subterranean train line connecting a series of forts

Barbed wire entanglements

Tank barricade

Heavy artillery pillbox

Machine-gun nest

Soldiers' quarters

Officers' quarters

Stores

Telephone bureau

Movies

Gym

Entrance via sunken road

Anti-aircraft guns

Hospital

Aircraft hangars

Medicine supplies

Air-conditioned fortress (air pressure raised to keep gas out)

Ammunition stores

Subway train

Garage

Here is a section of the claustrophobic interior of the Maginot Line. The fortifications were expensive and would prove to be a total failure.

Avoiding another war

After the First World War, the French government made plans to protect the country from another attack. They built a great line of tank barricades, machine-gun posts and concrete fortifications, known as the Maginot Line, along their border.

Despite these precautions, few people believed that another conflict could be brewing so soon after the last. Some people in France and Britain, including the future King Edward VIII, openly admired Hitler. British newspapers, such as the *Daily Mail*, even praised the new German leaders for providing a 'bulwark against communism' and for their success in combatting unemployment.

"We are a rich and vulnerable empire, and there are plenty of poor adventurers not very far away who look upon us with hungry eyes."

British Prime Minister Neville Chamberlain, 1938

Inside Hitler's Germany

Explaining his plans for Germany in his political manifesto
Mein Kampf – meaning My Struggle – Hitler wrote, "Every activity
and every need of every individual will be regulated... The time
of personal happiness is over." He was as good as his word.

The Nazis organized massive rallies all over Germany. Hitler was so effective at captivating a crowd that his propaganda minister Joseph Goebbels said that on these occasions, "The little worm turns into a huge dragon."

The biggest rallies were held every year at Nuremberg, the headquarters of the Nazi Party. Some were attended by over half a million people.

Young girls were supposed to join the League of Maidens, where they were taught first aid and how to be good Nazi wives and mothers. They also helped to raise funds for Nazi causes.

German boys had to join an organization called the Hitler Youth, where they received military training and were indoctrinated in Nazi politics.

Every means of receiving information, from cinema and radio, to newspapers and teaching at school, came under Nazi control. The belief that the Jews were responsible for all of Germany's problems was repeated constantly.

This book, *The Poisonous Mushroom,* warned German children not to trust their Jewish classmates.

This poster advertizes a 'documentary' movie called *The Eternal Jew* – a vicious piece of anti-Jewish propaganda, released in 1940.

Newspapers with anti-Jewish slogans were pinned up in public places for all to read.

Germany's Jews were persecuted or imprisoned, and made to carry out menial tasks, such as scrubbing the streets.

Half of the country's 500,000 Jews fled abroad before the War began.

On the night of November 9-10, 1938, there was a violent series of attacks on Jews all over Germany and Austria. It was known as *Kristallnacht*, or 'the Night of Broken Glass'. Jewish homes, shops and synagogues were ransacked or set on fire.

Hitler's lieutenants

"Naturally, the common people don't want war... But the people can always be brought to the bidding of leaders. That is easy. All you have to do is tell them they are being attacked."

Hermann Göring,
Reich Marshal

"The Jews have brought so much misery to our continent that the severest punishment meted out to them is still too mild..."

Joseph Goebbels,
Propaganda Minister,
Diary, April 27, 1942

Victorious Japanese troops
on the city walls of Nanking

"Let us have a
dagger between our
teeth, a bomb in
our hands and an
infinite scorn in
our hearts."

Benito Mussolini, 1928

The Axis Pact

When Mussolini's troops
invaded Abyssinia (see right),
there was an international
outcry, which brought Italy
closer to Germany. In 1936,
the two countries signed a
treaty of friendship, which
became known as the
'Rome-Berlin Axis', or 'the
Axis Pact'. Japan joined
in 1940, and the three
countries were referred to
as the 'Axis Powers'.

Mussolini makes
a speech,
surrounded
by his
generals.

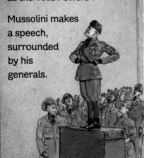

Steps to war

Those who had lived through the First World War
hoped that another war could be avoided. But that
hope was soon to fade.

Chaos reigned in China during the 1930s, as
rival warlords fought to dominate the country. In
1931, the Japanese invaded and occupied the
Chinese province of Manchuria. Protests from the
League of Nations were ignored, and by 1937
Japan was at war with the rest of China too. The
Japanese campaign was fought with appalling
cruelty. When the city of Nanking was occupied,
Japanese soldiers killed up to 200,000 civilians.

Italian adventures

In 1935-1936, the Italian army invaded Abyssinia
(now Ethiopia), one of the last independent
countries in Africa. Once again, protests by the
League of Nations were ignored. Mussolini's
army took eight months to defeat Emperor Haile
Selassie's poorly-equipped barefoot soldiers. This
should have warned Mussolini that his army was
ill-prepared to fulfil his dreams of conquest.

Germany grows stronger

As Hitler's confidence grew, he began to flaunt the terms of the Treaty of Versailles that had so humiliated his country two decades before. Most alarming of all, Germany started to build up its armament factories, providing work for millions of men made jobless by the Depression.

In 1936, German soldiers marched into the Rhineland and in 1938 Austria was absorbed into Germany. Both actions had been forbidden by the Treaty. Later that year, Hitler began to demand that the Sudetenland, a German-speaking part of Czechoslovakia (see map on page 25), should be absorbed into Germany.

This was unacceptable to Britain and France and they prepared for war. But, in September that year, Hitler met the British and French prime ministers, Neville Chamberlain and Edouard Daladier, at Munich and agreed a compromise (see right).

Sadly, it was a compromise that wasn't worth the paper it was printed on.

Appeasing Hitler

At Munich in September 1938, Britain and France agreed Germany could have the Sudetenland – in return for 'no more territorial demands'. Chamberlain came home with a document signed by Hitler, announcing 'peace in our time'.

Supporters of 'appeasement' saw it as giving the Germans territory that was rightfully theirs. Its opponents saw it as giving in to bullying.

Six months later, Hitler occupied the rest of the Czech lands. Appeasement had failed.

German troops march through the gates of Hradschin Castle, Prague, during the occupation of the Czech capital on March 15, 1939.

German tanks invading Poland,
September 1, 1939

Chapter 2

Outbreak

The Second World War began in a blaze of treachery and ruthless destruction. At first, the conflict was confined to the continent of Europe. But, in just over two years, most of the world had been dragged into a great struggle between two mighty alliances. This was to be a war where civilians, caught between merciless political opponents, would suffer far worse than the combatants.

The bomb aimer in a German Heinkel 111 looks down on an enemy town during the invasion of Poland in September 1939.

Dunkirk

As Hitler swept through Europe (see map, right), British and French forces found themselves trapped in the French port of Dunkirk. German forces were poised to destroy them, but Hitler ordered them to hold back.

In this lull in the fighting, hundreds of ships and boats crossed the English Channel in May and June 1940. Over 300,000 British and French soldiers were rescued.

Why did Hitler hold back? Some think he wanted to make peace with the British and didn't want to humiliate them; others that he was relying on his air force to finish the job later.

Europe enslaved

War broke out on September 1, 1939. It was a beautiful late-summer day and the ground was baked hard – perfect for the German tanks that rolled across the Polish border. Although the Polish army was larger than the invading German force, its troops were not as well trained or equipped. Within a week the Germans stood on the outskirts of Warsaw, the Polish capital.

Cities, towns and villages were bombed. Civilians, desperate to escape, clogged the roads and stopped Polish troops from reaching the front. In a secret agreement reached in the Nazi-Soviet Pact, the Russians and Germans had planned to split Poland between them. The Russians invaded Poland on September 17, Warsaw surrendered on September 27 and fighting was over by October 5. The country had fallen in little over a month.

Turning West

After Poland, there was an uneasy lull in the fighting. For several months, the French and British who had declared war on September 3, 1939, held back. Having seen how easily his army had overpowered the Poles, Hitler hoped his enemies would make peace. But that peace never came.

In April 1940, German forces attacked Norway and Denmark. Denmark fell in hours. The Norwegians held out until June 9. In May, Hitler turned his attention to Western Europe. His forces invaded the Netherlands and Belgium, then pushed into France, bypassing the Maginot Line.

Led by their greatest tank commander, General Heinz Guderian, German troops reached the English Channel in just over a week. The Allied armies crumbled and France surrendered. The campaign had lasted less than six weeks.

Hitler's revenge

At the end of the First World War, Germany had surrendered to France in a railway carriage in Compiègne Forest.

Hitler ordered the same carriage to be used to take the French surrender in June 1940.

The carriage was displayed in Berlin, but destroyed in 1945 – just as the city was about to fall into Allied hands at the end of the War.

Map of Europe in Summer, 1940

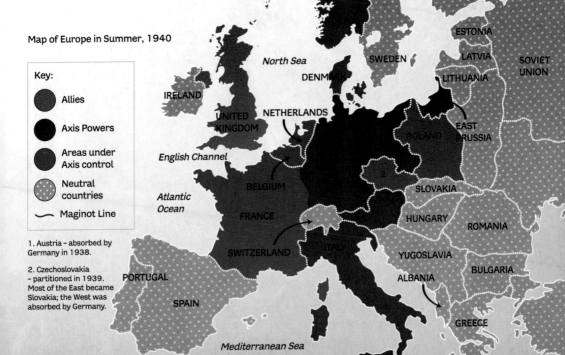

Key:

- Allies
- Axis Powers
- Areas under Axis control
- Neutral countries
- Maginot Line

1. Austria – absorbed by Germany in 1938.

2. Czechoslovakia – partitioned in 1939. Most of the East became Slovakia; the West was absorbed by Germany.

ESTONIA
LATVIA
SOVIET UNION
North Sea
SWEDEN
DENMARK
LITHUANIA
IRELAND
UNITED KINGDOM
NETHERLANDS
EAST PRUSSIA
POLAND
English Channel
Atlantic Ocean
BELGIUM
SLOVAKIA
FRANCE
HUNGARY
ROMANIA
SWITZERLAND
ITALY
YUGOSLAVIA
PORTUGAL
ALBANIA
BULGARIA
SPAIN
GREECE
Mediterranean Sea

Blitzkrieg

The tactic that enabled the Germans to conquer most of Europe was known as *Blitzkrieg*, or 'lightning war'. It was invented as a means of avoiding the stalemate of trench warfare that had cost so many lives in the First World War.

In the twenty years between the two wars, technology had moved on. The new attack weapons were formidable, making *Blitzkrieg* a fearsomely effective tactic. Here's how it worked:

1. Squadrons of heavy bombers flew deep behind enemy lines, destroying airbases, fuel and ammunition dumps, train stations and military headquarters.

2. Next, dive bombers screamed down to bomb or machine-gun front-line troops, creating terror and confusion among civilians fleeing from the fighting.

3. In some battles, soldiers were parachuted behind the front line, to carry out surprise attacks.

Blitzkrieg's fatal flaw

The initial success of *Blitzkrieg* gave great confidence to Germany's military commanders. But it worked best in the small-scale battlefields of Poland and Western Europe.

In the vast territory of the Soviet Union, it often took German foot soldiers days, rather than hours, to reach military installations pulverized by their aircraft and tanks. This gave Soviet troops time to regroup and organize further resistance.

4. Tanks and troop-carrying vehicles probed the enemy lines for weak spots. When they found them, they burst through. Then they attacked strongpoints from behind.

5. Before enemy troops could regroup, large numbers of foot soldiers followed the initial attacks, to kill or capture the soldiers who remained.

Cruel conquerors

The Nazis treated most of the countries they conquered with barbaric brutality. Their first victim, Poland, suffered such a cruel occupation that one in five citizens died – the highest percentage by population of any country caught up in the fighting.

Hitler had opened the campaign by telling his generals: "Close your hearts to pity. Whatever we find in the way of a leader class in Poland must be eliminated." It was Hitler's belief that Poles were *Untermenschen* – sub humans – fit only for slavery. Teachers, military officers, churchmen and political leaders were executed in their thousands.

When the Germans later invaded the Soviet Union in June 1941 (see pages 32-33), Soviet citizens were treated with similar cruelty. It is estimated that between 12 and 14 million Russian civilians died under Nazi occupation.

'Special Action'

Following close behind the soldiers of Germany's armies in Poland came *Einsatzgruppen* – Special Action Squads – whose grisly task it was to kill anyone they suspected of being a Jew or a communist.

In the early years of the War, some one and a half million people, mainly Jews, were murdered in this way. Sometimes tens of thousands were killed at a time, in massacres lasting several days.

Different rules

The citizens of France and Scandinavia were better treated. According to the Nazis' twisted racial philosophy, these people were worthy of more respect. Hitler admired the grandeur of Paris and saw Danes and Norwegians as 'racial comrades'. The Nazis even tried to recruit them to fight alongside their own soldiers.

But, no matter where they were from, men or women who attempted to rebel against Nazi rule almost certainly faced death.

Resistance

In Eastern Europe, particularly in occupied Soviet lands, large groups of soldiers carried on fighting against the Germans. These forces, known as partisans, hid in vast forests and grasslands, attacking German forces well away from the front line.

There was a terrible price to pay for such defiance. Resistance fighters faced certain death if captured. The Germans also held civilians as hostages.

These unlucky people would be murdered following any partisan activity. Sometimes entire villages were destroyed, along with their inhabitants.

Hitler, accompanied by senior German staff officers, surveys the soldiers who would build his new empire.

A squadron of Heinkel 111 bombers flies in close formation. These were slow, clumsy aircraft which made relatively easy targets for the RAF fighter pilots.

The Blitz

Between September 1940 and May 1941, London was bombed almost every night. Other cities, including Coventry and Liverpool, were also severely damaged.

Instead of causing panic and a collapse in morale, it made the British people all the more determined to fight on.

The Battle of Britain

From the French coast, the chalk cliffs of Dover can easily be seen across the English Channel. In the summer of 1940, this narrow stretch of water was all that stood between Hitler and the conquest of Britain. If the Germans could cross safely, the battered British army would be no match for the battle-hardened German soldiers.

A date was set for the invasion – September 15, 1940 – and the Germans cheerfully expected that fighting would be over by the time winter arrived. The invasion was given a codename: *Operation Sealion.*

But slow-moving boats packed with soldiers would make easy targets for the bombs and machine guns of British fighter aircraft. So first the Germans needed to win control of the sky.

Aerial attack

Hermann Goering, head of the German air force, the *Luftwaffe*, had a simple strategy to destroy the Royal Air Force, the RAF. He sent his aircraft to attack ships in the Channel, hoping to draw out British planes and shoot them down. But the plan backfired: the RAF shot down twice as many planes as the Germans. In response, the *Luftwaffe* started attacking airfields and destroying planes on the ground. Now they were winning.

The RAF tried a different approach: they bombed Berlin. Outraged, Hitler decided to stop the airfield raids and attack London and other cities instead.

During the Battle of Britain, as it became known, the *Luftwaffe* was defeated, plane by plane. They lost over 1,800 aircraft. The RAF, which included pilots from the Commonwealth and defeated eastern European nations, lost 900. Of 1,500 RAF pilots, around 400 were killed. But the bravery and skill of this small group meant that Hitler had to call off his invasion.

St. Paul's Cathedral towers over buildings still blazing from a night raid during the London Blitz.

RAF v. Luftwaffe

The RAF had several major advantages over the *Luftwaffe*.

• German planes had to make long journeys and could only stay a short while over England, or they would run out of fuel.

• Britain had a radar network, which meant they could tell when and where the Germans were coming.

• Many of the British planes could outfly German fighters and bombers.

• If they survived, RAF pilots shot down over the battle areas could fly again that very day. But surviving *Luftwaffe* pilots were usually captured.

"The gratitude of every home in our Island goes out to the British airmen who, undaunted by odds, unwearied in their constant challenge and mortal danger, are turning the tide of the World War... Never in the field of human conflict was so much owed by so many to so few."

British Prime Minister Winston Churchill, radio broadcast, August 20, 1940

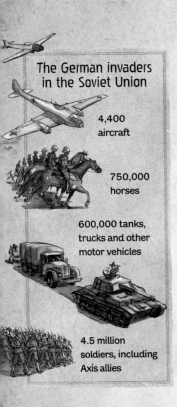

The German invaders in the Soviet Union

4,400 aircraft

750,000 horses

600,000 tanks, trucks and other motor vehicles

4.5 million soldiers, including Axis allies

German assault troops repel an attack by a Soviet tank, early in the German invasion of the Soviet Union.

Operation Barbarossa

The most ambitious invasion in history began on a misty June morning in 1941. German troops, and their Axis allies, advanced with thousands of tanks and planes across a vast border into the Soviet Union. Their mission was to destroy Soviet military power and seize the European part of the Soviet Union. This was the '*Lebensraum*' Hitler believed was Germany's to claim. The plan was codenamed *Barbarossa*, after a medieval German emperor.

A great, green sea

Axis forces stormed the country, from the north, the south and the middle. To the Germans who looked over the vast fields of grass that made up the Russian steppes, it looked as if they were crossing a great, green sea. Within a few months, the cities of Odessa, Kiev, Smolensk and Kursk had fallen.

Russia on the brink

By early October, Leningrad (now St. Petersburg) and Moscow, the two main Russian cities, were both under siege. Soviet losses had been appalling.

In the first weeks of the operation, 14,000 Soviet planes had been destroyed. By the end of the year, four and a half million Soviet soldiers had been killed or captured, and 75 million Soviet citizens were living under German rule.

The Germans had yet to take Leningrad and Moscow, but Hitler was confident the operation would be a success. "We have only to kick down the door and the whole rotten structure will come tumbling down," he had boasted. But one German battalion commander came closer to the truth. He quietly confided to a fellow officer that this invasion would be, "the worst disaster of German history."

"Immediately I had the feeling as if a monster was approaching slowly, threatening, frightening everyone to death..."

Moscow housewife Elena Skriyabina, June 22, 1941, on hearing of the invasion

Strange bedfellows

Before Hitler attacked Russia, Britain and the USA had regarded the vast communist empire with suspicion. But now they had a common cause.

British Prime Minister Churchill explained his support for Stalin by saying: "If Hitler invaded Hell I would at least make a favourable reference to the Devil..."

The Winter War

So certain was Hitler that his soldiers would defeat the Soviet Union well before winter, no plans were made for fighting in conditions of extreme cold.

But, as the Germans prepared to take Moscow, heavy snow fell and men froze to death in their thin summer uniforms. Improvizing as best they could, soldiers wrapped themselves in tablecloths, blankets and newspapers. Their guns were often too cold to work, and the engines of tanks and trucks froze up.

There was another problem. The Germans had fought with skill and conquered vast stretches of land, but the Russians seemed no closer to accepting defeat.

Leningrad

In September 1941, the Russian city of Leningrad was surrounded by German forces. What followed was a three-year ordeal, in which the city was starved and bombarded. People were so hungry that some feared they might be seized and eaten by fellow citizens. In winter, the ground froze so hard it was impossible to bury the dead. But Leningrad remained undefeated.

The siege finally came to an end in January 1944, when the Germans were driven back west. Nearly a million Leningrad citizens had died.

German soldiers brave the intense cold of a Russian winter.

The rewards of cruelty

The way the Germans treated civilians in occupied countries was beginning to work against them.

In parts of the Soviet Union, such as the Baltic states and the Ukraine, German soldiers had at first been welcomed as 'liberators' by people who saw themselves as independent nations under Russian control. They had even been greeted by cheering crowds offering them bread, salt and flowers.

But this jubilation was short-lived. The local people soon discovered that the Germans saw them as fit only for death or slavery. Resistance grew. As stories of massacres and brutality reached the rest of the Soviet Union, people began to rally around their previously unpopular government.

The struggle against their German conquerors became known in the Soviet Union as 'the Great Patriotic War', and the Soviet people would fight it with extraordinary bravery and determination.

These Leningrad citizens have become homeless after their apartment block was destroyed by German bombers.

"In summer, we picked up grass, boiled it, and ate it. Food was on our minds all the time... All the days became one long day and night. Imagine nine hundred such days."

A citizen of Leningrad looks back on the siege.

Pearl Harbor

7:50am, December 7, 1941: the US Navy base of Pearl Harbor, headquarters of the Pacific Fleet, is quiet. Great battleships lie spread out in the sheltered inlet by Pearl City, Oahu, Hawaii. The men on board, having a Sunday morning sleep, are disturbed by the low throb of aircraft engines. All at once come explosions and screams, machine-gun fire and the smell of burning oil.

The Japanese launched this surprise attack from six aircraft carriers, positioned 450km (280 miles) to the north. Miniature submarines slipped into the port too, launching torpedoes at their unsuspecting targets. Almost entirely unopposed, the Japanese planes wreaked terrible destruction. Ninety percent of the damage sustained during the strike occurred in the first 10 minutes.

Pearl Harbor losses

American

2,335 men

18 warships sunk or damaged

180 planes lost

121 planes damaged

Japanese

70 men

20 planes lost

74 planes damaged

The US fleet lies burning in Pearl Harbor. The battleship on the right is *USS Arizona*, in which a thousand men died.

The United States enters the War

Silence returned as quickly as it had been shattered. Then, half an hour later, came a second strike. This time the Americans were ready. Anti-aircraft guns and American fighter planes counter-attacked. The second strike was much less effective.

Nonetheless, the US Pacific Fleet had been dealt a near-fatal blow. Over 2,300 Americans had been killed, a thousand in a single huge explosion aboard the battleship *USS Arizona*.

Most Americans hadn't wished to get involved in the War – but the Pearl Harbor attack changed that. For Britain there was even better news: Hitler now declared war on the United States.

US President Franklin D. Roosevelt sent a message to Britain's Prime Minister Winston Churchill: "Today all of us are in the same boat… and it is a ship that will not and cannot be sunk."

The doomed admiral

The man who planned the attack, Admiral Isoroku Yamamoto, never approved of his government's decision to go to war.

Yamamoto had spent time in the USA and knew first-hand that Japan's new enemy was powerful and resourceful. When congratulated on the success of the Pearl Harbor attack he replied, "Gentlemen, we have just kicked a rabid dog."

Yamamoto was killed in 1943, when his plane was ambushed by US aircraft over the Solomon Islands.

A squad of British soldiers surrenders to the Japanese and is taken prisoner at Singapore.

A new Pacific empire

With the US reeling from the shock of Pearl Harbor, the Japanese acted quickly to seize the territory they coveted in Southeast Asia. Yamamoto had promised Japan's military rulers, "a wild six months to a year" before the US military could recover sufficiently to prevent further Japanese conquests.

The Japanese were aware that the United States was a much stronger military power. But their strategy was to resist a counter-attack so fiercely that the Americans would be forced to accept Japan's new position as ruler of the Eastern Pacific.

The Japanese made many of their prisoners do hard, physical work, such as building railways, but gave them very little food. A quarter of British prisoners died in captivity.

No time to lose

The Japanese wasted no time. In temporary command of the air and sea, their well-trained, battle-hardened troops swiftly occupied the Philippines, Malaya, Thailand and Burma. In India and Australia, people anxiously braced themselves for invasion. They had much to fear.

But the Japanese were so successful that they began to take risks – stretching their resources to breaking point by seizing New Guinea, some islands in the central Pacific, and even the chain of Aleutian Islands off the west coast of Alaska.

Meanwhile, in the USA, the Americans were nursing their wounds and preparing to hit back. Japan's brief moment as a military superpower was about to be dealt a powerful blow.

"Prisoner of war life changes you. You learn not to get too close to someone because the next day they could be dead. I suppose that was why I never married. I could never let myself care too much."

British soldier Charles Cleal, looks back on his wartime experiences.

Quoted in *The Guardian* newspaper, 2007.

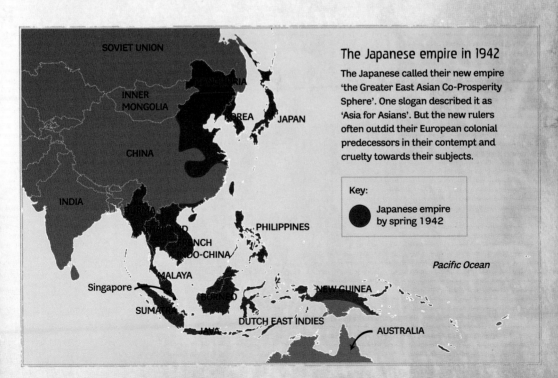

The Japanese empire in 1942

The Japanese called their new empire 'the Greater East Asian Co-Prosperity Sphere'. One slogan described it as 'Asia for Asians'. But the new rulers often outdid their European colonial predecessors in their contempt and cruelty towards their subjects.

Key:

● Japanese empire by spring 1942

SOVIET UNION
INNER MONGOLIA
MANCHURIA
KOREA
JAPAN
CHINA
INDIA
BURMA
THAILAND
FRENCH INDO-CHINA
PHILIPPINES
MALAYA
Singapore
BORNEO
SUMATRA
NEW GUINEA
DUTCH EAST INDIES
JAVA
AUSTRALIA
Pacific Ocean

This haunting image by Soviet photographer Dimitri Baltermants shows the aftermath of a massacre carried out by retreating German forces.

Chapter 3

The world turned upside down

The War affected the world like no other conflict in history. For the warring nations, every aspect of life, from science and industry to employment and trade, was harnessed to help with the war effort. And civilians in occupied nations would often suffer even more than the armed forces.

War at sea

From the balmy Pacific to the chilly North Atlantic, the oceans of the world became vast battlegrounds for mighty battleships and aircraft carriers. These acted as guardians of troop carriers and supply ships. Without their protection, it would have been impossible to ferry the millions of troops from their homelands to fight on the battlefields of Europe, Africa and Asia.

A crucial part of the War was the battle between cargo ships and submarines. US factories produced huge quantities of weapons for the Allies, especially Britain and the Soviet Union, which had to be transported by merchant ships across hostile waters to reach their destinations. The cargo ship's greatest enemy was the submarine, and the submariners of the German navy were particularly effective.

Life in a submarine

Life on a submarine was very tough, but there were plenty of recruits. Men volunteered out of a sense of duty or for extra pay.

Voyages would last from six to eight weeks, with no chance of a shower or clean laundry.

Conditions were cramped and airless, with men sleeping like sardines next to engines, pumps and torpedoes.

At first, the German submarines appeared to be winning the Battle of the Atlantic (see opposite) and their crews were hailed as heroes in Germany.

But, by 1945, being a submariner had become one of the most dangerous jobs of the War. Two out of three submarines were sunk and 30,000 of the 40,000 submariners in the German navy lost their lives. No other combat units in the War suffered comparable losses.

The Battle of the Atlantic

The German *Unterseeboote*, or U-boats, mainly operated from the Atlantic ports of occupied France. Sometimes they went out in groups of six or seven, known as 'wolf packs', to search for and destroy Allied shipping.

On one October night in 1940, for example, they sank 20 of 35 cargo ships from Convoy SC7, which were carrying much-needed weapons and supplies to Britain. Winston Churchill confessed that U-boats were the only thing that really frightened him, and Britain's survival depended on their defeat. He called this part of the War 'the Battle of the Atlantic'.

Defending the seaways

As the war wore on, new tactics were developed to protect cargo ships. At first, U-boats only attacked on the surface, and at night. Underwater, they could be detected using an early form of sound detection known as ASDIC. But when ships began to be fitted with the new technology of radar, subs on the surface became easier to spot. So they had to return to attacking from underwater, where it was more difficult to fire their torpedoes accurately.

A breakthrough came when British scientists cracked German codes, after an encoding machine was captured from a U-boat in May, 1941 (see page 46). After this, whenever a U-boat sent out coded signals about its location, Allied convoys were forewarned and had air and sea escorts ready to defend them.

"By midnight the whole area was in a state almost of daylight by the ships burning."

Lt. Robert Sherwood, British Royal Navy, recalls the night when Convoy SC7 lost 20 of its 35 ships.

An Allied destroyer escort drops a depth charge on a German submarine, which was attacking a convoy out in the Atlantic Ocean.

Women at war

During the Second World War, millions of women worked in factories, coal mines and steelworks, filling the places left by men called up to fight. But some also became willing or unwilling participants in the fighting itself.

The White Rose

One of the most famous women fighter pilots of the War was Russian pilot Lilya Litvak, who shot down 12 German planes, becoming the highest scoring woman 'ace'.

Small and pretty, she was nicknamed 'the White Rose', because she painted a new flower on the nose of her *Yak* fighter every time she shot down a German plane.

Famous for her daredevil moves, Lilya's fame eventually cost her her life. She was last seen hurtling through the sky with eight German fighters on her tail.

Stalin's female falcons

In the first year of the War, Soviet fighter pilots, known by the Soviet newspapers as 'Stalin's falcons', had a 50% chance of being killed. Such losses were unsustainable, so they were forced to accept female volunteers, many of whom had learned to fly in youth organizations. By the end of the War, more than one in ten Soviet combat pilots was a woman.

Lilya Litvak, far left, with two other women fighters – only the one on the right would survive the War.

French Resistance fighters, including a woman with a captured German sub-machine gun, stalk German troops in the liberation of Paris, August, 1944.

Women on the front line

In Eastern Europe, women were much closer to the fighting than their contemporaries in Britain and the USA. Russian women often fought alongside men on the front line, as well as taking part as snipers and combat pilots. Polish women joined in the fighting in the Warsaw Uprising of 1944 (see page 81). They also took part in partisan campaigns behind the lines.

British and American women joined up as nurses and ferry pilots and other auxiliary roles. But the only ones involved in the fighting were members of the Resistance, the secret underground organization that fought against German occupation in Europe.

The Nazis strongly disapproved of women taking on what they considered to be men's jobs. But towards the end of the war, even in Germany, women served with anti-aircraft batteries.

Violette Szabo

Violette Szabo was a young woman, half English and half French, whose husband had been killed in action. She was parachuted into France to fight with the French Resistance.

Captured after a gun fight with German soldiers, she was eventually executed in Ravensbruck Concentration Camp in 1945, alongside two other British women agents.

After her death, she won two awards for bravery: the George Cross and the French *Croix de Guerre*.

The science of warfare

During the Second World War, scientists worked around the clock to produce new weapons, machines and medicines. Scientific advances were made at a speed unimaginable in peacetime, as the development of new technology gave one side a crucial advantage over the other.

Before the War, the Germans developed a sophisticated coding device, known as ENIGMA, to transmit messages to generals and U-boat commanders. The code baffled the British who were desperate to discover when their ships were likely to be attacked.

But then the British captured an ENIGMA codebook from a U-boat, and invented a room-sized computer, called Colossus, which enabled them to master the codes. However, the Germans were so confident their codes couldn't be broken, that they continued to use them throughout the War.

The antibiotic penicillin was discovered in the late 1920s, but it wasn't until 1943 that US pharmaceutical company Merck & Co developed a technique to produce it on a large scale.

By June 1944, 2.3 million doses had been prepared to treat soldiers wounded in battle.

The first operational jet fighter, the German *Messerschmitt Me-262*, was way ahead of its time. It was faster than any Allied plane, but was only introduced in 1944 and relatively few were produced.

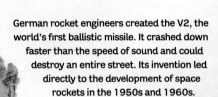

German rocket engineers created the V2, the world's first ballistic missile. It crashed down faster than the speed of sound and could destroy an entire street. Its invention led directly to the development of space rockets in the 1950s and 1960s.

Tanks, planes and trucks need vast quantities of fuel, but the Germans had no supplies of their own, except coal. So German chemical engineers devised a technique to produce synthetic petroleum from coal. By 1944, chemical plants were producing at least half the fuel needed for the war effort.

The most important invention of the War was probably the atomic bomb, which brought a swift end to the conflict in August 1945.

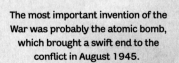

It was developed in the USA as a result of a secret project, codenamed *Manhattan*, and tested in the desert in New Mexico, USA.

Death from above

Aircraft technology had made huge leaps since the First World War. Flimsy biplanes had been replaced by sleek, speedy fighters and sturdy four-engine bombers that could carry 6,300kg (14,000lbs) or more of high explosive bombs.

Europe was haunted by the prospect of bombing. Governments feared it would cause mass panic, leading to a breakdown of law and order, seriously damaging a country's ability to wage war.

But, when war came in 1939, these fears were only partly realized. The *Luftwaffe* did terrible damage to great cities such as Warsaw, Rotterdam and London. But it seemed to make people even more determined to fight on.

A Nazi official oversees soldiers helping to clear up the damage following the destruction of Hamburg in the summer of 1943.

Reaping the whirlwind

As the war turned against the Axis, German cities such as Hamburg and Dresden suffered unimaginable destruction. Allied bombers used a combination of small incendiary bombs and high explosives. The attacks were so fierce they created a vast firestorm, causing powerful winds that sucked people into its core. In Japan, Tokyo had half its buildings destroyed.

The bombers faced daunting odds too. Anti-aircraft guns on the ground fired shells, known as 'flak', that exploded around them. The lumbering bombers were also easy targets for nimble fighter aircraft. Nearly half of all Allied bomber crews were killed. For those on the most dangerous missions, perhaps only one in thirty survived.

"The Nazis entered this war under the rather childish delusion that they were going to bomb everyone else, and nobody was going to bomb them. They sowed the wind, and now they are going to reap the whirlwind."

Sir Arthur Harris,
Head of British Bomber Command

Dresden destroyed

In February 1945, the RAF attacked Dresden in one of the most infamous air raids of the War. The city was packed with refugees, and at least 25,000 civilians (mainly women and children) were killed. The heart of the old city was almost completely destroyed.

The RAF maintained that Dresden was a legitimate target because it was a transport hub and had several armaments factories. But many commentators saw the raid as a 'war crime'.

Industry goes to war

> "Long Beach was a military town. There were several parades a year. We'd have miles and miles of tanks driving down Pine Avenue and everyone standing and cheering and waving flags. It was a constant reminder of this mighty strength and everything was going to be all right."
>
> Californian munitions worker Sheril Cunning, quoted in *The Good War* by Studs Terkel

For any country at war, the struggle to produce weapons, shells, bombs and ammunition is just as important as the fighting ability of their troops. Hitler's biggest mistake was to fight three of the greatest industrial powers in the world. The fact that they could manufacture more tanks, ships and aircraft than the Axis powers ensured, more than anything else, that the Allies would win the war.

The United States produced more weapons than any other country. Even before they joined the War in 1941, the Americans were supplying armaments to Britain and the Soviet Union. Between 1940 and 1945, they managed to produce a staggering 200,000 combat aircraft.

Far away from the threat of enemy attack, an American factory produces row upon row of gleaming B-17 Flying Fortress bombers.

Factories under fire

All the Allied powers employed women to work in armament factories – a resource that the Germans were slow to use. And American factories had a unique advantage in the war – they were too far away from the combat zones to be threatened by enemy bombing.

Soviet factories, on the other hand, were often built close to the fighting. Their workers toiled in underground caverns or bunkers, producing tanks, aircraft and field guns that could be quickly transported to the front.

A Soviet munitions worker at work in a factory close to the front. Russian forces received armaments from both Britain and USA, but many of their most successful weapons were produced in their own factories.

The Allies tried to end the War by bombing Germany's armament factories. But the bombing was not as effective as they had hoped. Despite being under constant attack, German industrial production actually rose throughout 1944.

Slave workers

The Nazis didn't allow German women to take an active part in the war effort until the final stages of the War. They didn't like the idea of women working in factories. They believed in the 19th-century German saying: 'Children, Church and Kitchen' – describing the three roles most suitable for women.

Instead, the Germans filled their factories with slave workers from conquered territories.

While Allied factory workers felt their efforts were helping to keep their country free, Germany's workers performed their tasks half-heartedly, sometimes deliberately sabotaging goods or machinery.

The Nazis treated these workers with cruelty, threatening execution if they didn't perform well. They were often worked so hard, they collapsed and died.

Fighting for China

During the 1930s and 1940s, a war was being waged in China that was every bit as savage and destructive as the one being fought in Europe.

At the start of the 20th century, China had entered a period of upheaval, with the collapse of the 300-year-old Qing dynasty. By the early 1930s, China was nominally ruled by the Nationalist Party, led by Chiang Kai-shek. But the Nationalists were fighting against the Chinese communists, led by Mao-Zedong, as well as various regional warlords.

The Japanese threat

China also faced a threat from Japan, whose leaders regarded China as a prime source of raw materials, with a vast workforce to be exploited, and as a ready market for Japanese goods. From the early 1930s until the end of the War, Japan pitted its powerful and well-trained army against the ill-equipped and poorly-trained Chinese.

Japan's cruellest war

Japanese forces were notorious for behaving with cruelty – nowhere more so than in China, whose people they had long regarded as inferior.

Inhabitants of conquered cities, such as Nanking, suffered rape and murder on a massive scale. Poison gas was regularly used too – the only battlefield use of this weapon during the War.

Japanese aircraft even dropped containers of fleas infected with bubonic plague on Chinese cities.

Japanese soldiers, wearing masks to protect them from the gas they use against their Chinese enemy, in Shanghai, 1937

Here, Japanese soldiers are preparing to take the city of Nanking. In the days that followed, up to 200,000 Nanking citizens were murdered.

'The Three Alls'

Japan's military leaders boasted they could conquer the country in three months. But China was too large and populous for an easy victory. Although the Japanese won control of the Chinese province of Manchuria, in addition to coastal regions, key cities and rail networks, the vast interior remained in the hands of hostile Chinese forces.

The Chinese fought with ruthless determination, deliberately flooding huge areas of land as they fell into Japanese hands. Mounting Japanese losses, and failure to gain control, led the Japanese generals to introduce a new strategy. It was known as 'The Three Alls': kill all, loot all and burn all.

The cost of war

As China was in a state of chaos, it's impossible to obtain accurate casualty figures. But the Chinese may have suffered as many as 20 million dead and wounded, and up to 95 million who became homeless.

As this poster shows, the US provided aid to help China in the struggle against Japan.

From War to civil war

By the time the War ended in 1945, Chinese forces were slowly gaining the upper hand. As the Japanese withdrew, the Nationalists and communists turned their attention to each other, in the final stage of a civil war that ended in a victory for the Chinese Communist Party in 1949.

The Holocaust

"We are going
to destroy the
Jews... The day
of reckoning
has come."

Hitler in conversation
with Czech diplomat
Frantisek Chvalkovsky,
January 21, 1939

At the heart of Hitler's view of the world was hatred
of Jews, who he blamed for Germany's economic
woes. At first, the Nazis imagined they would be
able to expel their Jewish citizens to live in other
countries. But as the war closed borders and
Germany took over most of Europe, this became
impractical. So, instead, Jews were herded into
specific areas of cities, known as ghettoes.

In early 1942, Nazi officials gathered at a
conference in a villa by the lake at Wannsee, near
Berlin, where they came up with a shocking plan.
They would build 'death camps' where Jews would
be sent to be gassed – a more efficient method
than shooting, which was too 'messy' and too
public. The Nazis called this 'the Final Solution to
the Jewish Question'.

Jews arrive at Auschwitz
in cattle trucks and are
immediately selected for
work or extermination.
The men in striped
uniforms are prisoners
chosen to help the guards.

Hitler's hangmen

Here are three of the principal architects of the Final Solution.

Heinrich Himmler, chief of the S.S. (military wing of the Nazi Party). He thought up the Final Solution, describing it as 'a glorious chapter that has not and will not be spoken of'.

Reinhard Heydrich was chief of the Main German S.S. Office and chairman of the Wannsee Conference. Even his colleagues referred to him as 'the blond beast'.

Adolf Eichmann organized the mass deportation of Jews to the death camps. He referred to the Jews living in ghettoes as 'a storage problem'.

Death factory

Jews arrived at Auschwitz by train. At the railway siding, most women and children were sent to be killed in the gas chambers.

Men and healthier women were selected for work in factories until they were too weak to continue.

Those selected for death were told they were to have a shower. Their heads were shaved, and the hair kept for use in mattresses or as insulation and soundproofing in U-boats and aircraft.

Clothes, shoes and spectacles were sent to Germany. Gold teeth and wedding rings were removed after death to be melted down.

In the gas chambers, victims were gassed with Zyklon B cyanide. Bodies were burned and the ashes were used as fertilizer.

The death camps

The death camps were built in occupied Poland, at the heart of Nazi-controlled Europe. Jews all across Europe – from Norway to the Caucasus – were shipped by freight train to camps such as Treblinka, Sobibor, Belzec and Chelmno. The most deadly of all was Auschwitz-Birkenau, where over a million people died between 1942 and 1944.

Jews were told they were going to be 'resettled'. A few knew what this really meant and went into hiding. Others rebelled. But, in all, between five and a half and six million people were murdered for being Jewish. This mass murder has become known as 'the Holocaust', a word that comes from the ancient Greek, meaning 'sacrifice by fire'.

Propaganda: truth and lies

During the War, governments on both sides used propaganda
— information designed to boost morale or to encourage people
to support the war effort. But at times the intention was to try to
influence or confuse the enemy. In an age before television or the
internet, news and opinions were shaped by newspapers, radio and
posters, as well as newsreels and feature films shown in cinemas.

THEY'RE WATCHING US...
PLENTY!

PUT *ALL* YOUR POWER IN THE JOB!

DODGE

This American poster
uses images of the
three Axis leaders to
encourage US factory
workers to produce
more war goods.

Governments
warned people that
spies were listening.

Ganz Deutschland
hört den Führer

mit dem Volksempfänger

This Nazi poster announces : "All of Germany
listens to the Führer with the People's Radio."
Speeches by leading Nazis such as Goebbels,
the Propaganda Minister, boosted
the morale of Germany's war
weary population.

In the days before
widespread TV, families
would all gather
around the radio.

This British poster exhorts women to help with the war effort by working in factories producing armaments. The American government produced similar posters.

Some women worked as air raid wardens.

This poster celebrates the Japanese success at Pearl Harbor. It was produced in Fascist Italy. The flags of the three Axis powers fly in the background.

A Soviet soldier kills a Nazi snake distorted into the shape of a swastika, the symbol of the Nazi Party. It reads: "Death to the Fascist Beast!"

Russians dropped propaganda leaflets over German troops.

Under attack from Japanese machine-gun fire, US soldiers wade towards a beach on Makin Atoll in the Gilbert Islands, in November 1943.

Chapter 4

Axis in retreat

By 1942, Hitler's new empire stretched from Norway
to the borders of Soviet Central Asia. In the Pacific,
Australians braced themselves for a Japanese invasion.
But the Axis powers had overreached themselves.
In the Soviet Union and Eastern Europe, Hitler's armies
suffered crushing defeats, in battles that cost the lives of
millions of soldiers. In the Pacific, the Japanese soon discovered
just how powerful their American opponent really was.

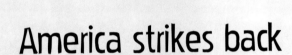

A US Dauntless dive bomber drops its bomb. Planes like this, launched from aircraft carriers, were to become the future of navy warfare.

America strikes back

So successful was the Japanese assault on the Pacific that by the spring of 1942 their commanders were considering invading Australia and the US territory of Hawaii – the scene of the infamous Pearl Harbor attack six months before.

Japanese military planners busily exchanged coded signals detailing fresh plans. Unfortunately for them, the Americans had cracked their code.

The Battle of Coral Sea

In early May, 1942, a Japanese fleet of 50 ships headed for the southern tip of New Guinea – a staging post for an attack on Australia. But the fleet was intercepted in the Coral Sea. Here, for the first time, an entire battle was fought with planes from aircraft carriers – neither side sighted the other's ships. The Japanese destroyed one aircraft carrier and 65 planes. But their own losses were almost double. The US were able to replace their ships and planes, but for Japan it was a serious setback.

Pacific battleground

The Battles of the Coral Sea and Midway (see right) showed that the United States had finally recovered from the disaster of Pearl Harbor. And they put an end to Japanese plans to expand their Pacific empire.

But, although the Japanese navy no longer ruled the Pacific seaways, they fought with grim determination to hold onto their newly-conquered empire.

Japan overreaches itself

Nevertheless, they pressed on with plans to conquer Hawaii, sending a massive invasion fleet to occupy the US naval base of Midway in the central Pacific.

Once again, US commanders intercepted radio signals so they knew exactly what the Japanese were planning. Admiral Yamamoto, who led Japan's fleet, hoped for a 'decisive battle' which would destroy US power once and for all.

The Battle of Midway

The battle began on the morning of June 4, 1942, when Yamamoto's fleet suffered a massive attack from aircraft from US airbases and carriers. In an extraordinary six minutes, three Japanese carriers – the *Kaga*, *Akagi* and *Soryu* – were set ablaze.

All three ships sank, and another, *Hiryu*, was sunk later that day. The US lost only one: *Yorktown*. Yamamoto's plan had failed: Japanese expansion came to an abrupt end.

USS *Yorktown* is shown here, irreparably damaged by Japanese bombs during the Battle of Midway. Within hours, this huge vessel will sink.

Life onboard

A carrier like the *Yorktown* held 90 aircraft and a crew of over 2,200 men. Life onboard was noisy and dangerous, especially for the men on the flight deck. They were in charge of arming the planes, fuel supplies, and take-off and landing.

Despite its huge size, *Yorktown* could travel over 23,000km (14,500 miles) – an equivalent distance by sea from London to Sydney, Australia – and had a top speed of 60kmph (37mph).

As if to demonstrate their invincibility, the US navy had a new aircraft carrier named *Yorktown* in action in the Pacific barely a year after the original carrier was sunk.

Crewmen in *Yorktown*'s hangar

The desert war

Desert warfare has a particular appeal to military leaders. With few towns or obstacles in the way, generals are free to move their forces at will. But such combat also brings great hardship for the soldiers involved – with the heat and cold of the desert, the lack of food or water, and the difficulty of navigating through featureless terrain.

Italy attacks

The desert war began in 1940, when Mussolini joined up with Germany and attacked Egypt (a British colony in all but name). But the attack failed and Allied forces turned on the Italian colonies of Libya, Abyssinia (Ethiopia) and Italian East Africa.

Hitler was forced to send troops to rescue his ally. The newly formed *Afrika Korps*, led by Erwin Rommel, one of the most capable generals of the War, pushed the British back into Egypt and threatened to occupy the entire North African coast.

Unwilling warriors

Within a couple of months of the attack on their African colonies (see right), 115,000 Italian soldiers had surrendered to a much smaller British and Commonwealth force.

The success caused the British foreign secretary Anthony Eden to quip, "Never has so much been surrendered by so many to so few." – an echo of Winston Churchill's famous phrase about the pilots of the Battle of Britain (see page 28).

In this painting of Allied troops in action, by war artist Will Longstaff, the tanks are larger than life – perhaps to emphasize their importance in the vast battlefields of the desert.

The Afrika Korps

In the first couple of years, boundaries were pushed back and forth between the two sides. But, in August 1942, the exhausted and demoralized Allied troops were revitalized by the appointment of a determined new commander, Bernard Montgomery, known as 'Monty'.

El Alamein

The turning point came at the second battle of the Egyptian desert town of El Alamein, in October 1942. The *Afrika Korps* had surrounded themselves with mines and booby traps. But, by the time of the attack, Rommel had been sent home, drained by months of intense fighting. The Germans also lacked air support – their planes had been diverted to the Soviet Union – which turned out to be a fatal flaw.

After an intense artillery bombardment, the Germans began to retreat. A month later, Allied forces landed in Morocco and Algeria. Caught in the middle, the Axis troops surrendered.

Two great generals

The resourceful and cunning Rommel, known as 'the Desert Fox', was a German war hero. Even Winston Churchill admitted he was a great general.

But after the Germans were defeated at El Alamein, Rommel's star waned. In 1944, he was implicated in a plot to kill Hitler and ordered to commit suicide.

A former junior officer during the First World War, Montgomery had witnessed appalling slaughter and was careful with the lives of his own soldiers.

But he also had a reputation among his fellow generals, and politicians who worked with him, of being a difficult man. Churchill described him as: "In defeat, unbeatable. In victory, unbearable."

The ordeal of Stalingrad

With Moscow and Leningrad still unconquered, Hitler ordered his soldiers to head south. Their prize was the oil fields of the Caucasus region, on the borders of Asia.

Throughout summer 1942, German troops, under the command of General Friedrich Paulus, gobbled up vast swathes of Soviet territory. In August, they closed in on the industrial city of Stalingrad – home to 400,000 people and an important transport hub for the region.

German attack

First, the Germans sent 600 aircraft to bomb the city. Although many people had already fled, around 40,000 civilians were killed in air raids and artillery bombardments at the start of the battle. But the Germans were sowing the seeds of their own destruction. As they churned the city into rubble, they created the ideal terrain for the defenders.

> "Our battalion plus tanks is attacking the grain elevator. The battalion is suffering heavy losses. The elevator is occupied not by men but by devils no bullets or flames can destroy."
>
> Diary of Private Wilhelm Hoffman, German 6th Army

Soviet soldiers advance through the rubble of Stalingrad, in sharp winter sunshine. Unlike their German opponents, they wear warm, winter uniforms.

German soldiers march through a blizzard. They were ill-prepared for the ferocious Russian winter.

Soviet resistance

A month passed, but still the Soviets resisted, often with extraordinary heroism, fighting room by room across the shattered carcass of the city.

In early October, Paulus mustered his strength for a final all-out assault. His men fought in terrible hand-to-hand combat among the tangled remains of steelworks and factories. The assault failed.

Freezing to death

As winter set in, the Germans were still fighting in summer uniforms. Outside Stalingrad, Soviet troops were targeting Germany's allies – Italians, Romanians and Hungarians left to hold territory around the city. When the Soviets attacked, these men quickly surrendered.

Within a week, Paulus's army was surrounded. Starved of supplies and unable to evacuate the wounded, the German army began to disintegrate, with men dying of frostbite or freezing to death. On February 2, they surrendered: 91,000 men were taken prisoner, but only 5,000 survived the War. The city they left behind was so devastated that barely one in a hundred buildings remained.

Death or surrender?

Near the end of the battle, Hitler promoted Paulus to field marshal. No German field marshal had ever been captured, so this was a clear message that he should commit suicide rather than surrender.

Paulus knew exactly what Hitler intended him to do. But he refused to oblige and surrendered instead.

Scorched Earth

The War in the East was fought more ferociously than in the West. When either side retreated, they destroyed anything the enemy could use – crops, livestock, buildings, bridges, railway lines...

By the end of the War, the Russians had lost nearly a third of their total wealth to battle damage. This deliberate policy of wanton destruction was known as 'Scorched Earth'.

The Battle of Kursk

Stalingrad dealt a crippling blow to German forces, but they were far from defeated. Barely a month later, they captured the city of Kharkov. Then another target presented itself: 300km (200 miles) north, three Soviet armies were defending the city of Kursk. German forces were in a strong position to encircle the city and crush them.

At this stage of the War, Soviet forces were well equipped with arms and tanks, and their soldiers were fighting with skill. But at Kursk the Germans had a deadly advantage: new tanks, the Panther and the Tiger, which were far superior to the standard Soviet tank, the T-34.

In July 1943, in the flat grasslands of the Russian steppes, the greatest tank battle in history began in torrential rain. More men and tanks were pitched against each other than in the entire Western European campaign of the next two years.

Soviet soldiers run to keep up with fast-moving tanks during the Battle of Kursk.

Winners and losers

Over the eight-day battle, over 90,000 men were killed or wounded. The Soviets lost 2,300 tanks; the Germans, 400. The Germans looked like winners. But, despite concentrating a third of their entire military strength around Kursk, they failed to break through the Soviets' defensive positions. The Soviets were producing tanks faster than the Germans could destroy them. In this grinding war of attrition, quantity was more important than quality.

Another blow

Meanwhile, thousands of miles away, in the warm, blue waters of the Mediterranean, Allied soldiers were landing in Sicily. Italy was being invaded. Hitler diverted some of his forces south, and the rest of the German army in the Soviet Union retired to regroup and repair. Over the next two years, the course of the War moved relentlessly against them.

Battle of the Titans

Here you can see a comparison between Soviet and German forces and equipment.

■ Soviet Union
■ Germany

Men
1,300,000
900,000

Tanks
3,600
2,700

Aircraft
2,400
2,000

Artillery guns
20,000
10,000

Italy's tragedy

Mussolini, accompanied by a German commando

Mussolini had dreamed of a new Roman empire, boasting of the Mediterranean as an 'Italian lake'. But Italian military exploits almost all ended in farce or defeat. During their first venture in Africa, the Italian Commander-in-Chief, Italo Balbo, was shot down and killed by his own anti-aircraft gunners. Italian soldiers were badly equipped and badly led. Many Italians hadn't wanted to fight alongside Hitler. At the end of his life, Hitler regarded his alliance with Italy as one of his greatest mistakes.

Up into Italy

After victories in North Africa, Allied troops invaded the Italian island of Sicily on July 10, 1943. It was conquered in five weeks. On September 3, they invaded the mainland, planning to work their way up north. The Italian government, already in secret talks with the Allies, signed a ceasefire and surrendered. Overnight, German troops in Italy changed from being Italy's allies to being an occupying force.

Allied artillery and aircraft reduce Monte Cassino to ruins in March, 1944. German forces had turned this historic town into a fortress.

Italian soldiers were disarmed by the Germans, but where possible they switched sides. By the end of the year, at least 350,000 of them were fighting alongside the Allies.

The mountains and rivers of Italy made it a difficult country to conquer. To speed things up, Allied commanders tried to land troops behind enemy lines along the coast. But landing craft for these assaults were often in short supply.

Allied breakthrough

A breakthrough came at Monte Cassino, an ancient hilltop monastery which the Germans had turned into a fortress. Polish, Indian and Nepalese Gurkha troops fought a gruelling battle alongside other Allies. The monastery was destroyed. After taking Monte Cassino, the Allies occupied Rome, which had been left undefended by the Germans, on June 4, 1944.

But the Allies' main priority soon shifted to France, and the Germans managed to hold onto the north of Italy until the end of the War.

Mussolini's end

Mussolini was captured and executed by Italian partisans (resistance fighters against the Germans) in April 1945.

His body, and that of his mistress, Clara Petacci, were hung up in the main square in Milan. They were spat at and shot at by Italians who had come to hate the man who had brought so much death and destruction to their country.

US war artist Dwight C. Shepler captures the horror of a *kamikaze* suicide attack on an aircraft carrier during the Pacific campaign.

War in the Pacific

Despite the defeats of Coral Sea and Midway, the Japanese remained masters of the eastern Pacific. Now their garrisons prepared to face the coming onslaught. They knew they could never match US military strength, but they hoped to inflict such huge casualties that the US would be forced to allow them to hold on to much of their new empire.

One soldier's war

"There was nothing macho about the war at all. We were a bunch of scared kids who had to do a job. The only way you could get it over with was to kill them off before they killed you. The war I knew was totally savage."

US GI E. B. Sledge, quoted in Studs Terkel's *The Good War*

Operation Cartwheel

The first thrust in the US campaign to dislodge the Japanese was codenamed *Operation Cartwheel*. General Douglas MacArthur was to lead his men through New Guinea and into the Philippines, and Admiral Chester Nimitz was to lead his troops through the Pacific islands and atolls of the Marshalls and Marianas.

The war in the Pacific was fought with unrelenting brutality. Allied soldiers soon discovered that their enemy was prepared to fight to the death. It was reported that wounded Japanese would even detonate grenades to kill enemy troops who came to offer medical aid.

In November 1943 at Betio, a tiny atoll in the Tarawa island chain, 5,000 Japanese fought so fiercely over three days that they killed 1,000 US soldiers, wounding 2,000 others.

Leyte Gulf

The Japanese gathered together a formidable fleet. At Leyte Gulf, on October 23-25, 1944, in an area of the Pacific the size of France, they fought the greatest sea battle in history. To lose meant certain defeat. As a mark of desperation, suicide pilots were used widely for the first time (see page 84).

But, overwhelmed by carrier aircraft, Japan lost 26 ships to the US's seven. Despite the hopelessness of their position, Japan's leaders were determined to keep fighting.

US Marines take cover during the fierce fighting on Tarawa. Only 17 of the 5,000 Japanese defending the island survived.

Death of a giant

Musashi – one of the two largest battleships of its day – was the most prominent Japanese casualty at Leyte Gulf.

It was 263m (863 ft) long and had a crew of 2,500.

Nine huge guns could fire 45cm (18 inch) shells, although the blast from the barrels sometimes killed crewmen nearby.

17 bombs and 19 torpedoes from US aircraft sent the *Musashi* and 1,023 of her crew to the bottom of the Pacific Ocean.

Back into Europe

In England, the Allies had spent the last two years building up troops and supplies to invade and liberate Western Europe from German occupation. US General Dwight Eisenhower was in charge of breaching the Germans' western fortifications. His problem was where, when and how quickly?

Calais, so close it could be seen from the cliffs of Dover, was the obvious choice, but it was heavily defended. So he chose Normandy. This involved a much longer sea crossing, but it had plenty of flat beaches, ideal for putting large numbers of men and vehicles ashore quickly. And its position meant that an assault could be launched from all along the English coast.

A three-pronged attack

Speed was essential. Eisenhower planned to land men in landing craft, in gliders and by parachute. The more he could land on the first day, the more difficult it would be for the Germans to drive his soldiers back into the sea.

US troops wade out to face machine-gun fire on *Omaha* beach. Over a thousand of them would die here.

Omaha Beach is shown here the day after the invasion. Eisenhower's plan was that the Allies should land as many men and supplies as possible in the first few days.

D-Day

The invasion, codenamed *Operation Overlord*, began in the early hours of June 6, 1944 – or *D-Day*. British glider troops landed near Caen to secure roads and bridges into the city. Airborne landings continued through the night. French Resistance groups sabotaged train lines and radio stations, to hinder the German response.

At 6:30am on June 6, the first men came ashore at the US landing zone codenamed *Utah* (see map). By nightfall, 150,000 soldiers had arrived in Normandy. Miraculously, only 2,500 were killed.

The worst casualties were at *Omaha*, where over 1,000 US soldiers were killed trying to reach German gun emplacements in the cliffs above the beach. The fighting grew fiercer when German reinforcements arrived, but by then the Allied troops were too strongly entrenched to be driven out. By the end of June, over 850,000 of them had landed in France.

The landing beaches

The largest seaborne invasion force ever assembled stormed into Normandy on D-Day. It was made up of men from many different Allied nations. The majority were US, British and Canadian, but there were French and Commonwealth soldiers too.

The Normandy Landings took place on five separate beaches: codenamed *Omaha* and *Utah* (US), *Gold* and *Sword* (British) and *Juno* (Canadian).

Children at war

Civilians were caught up in the fighting in greater numbers than in any other conflict in history. Aerial bombardment brought death and destruction to families hundreds of miles away from the battlefields. For some children, especially in countries spared from occupation, the war was an exciting interlude. But for most, it would be remembered as a time of fear, hunger and tragedy.

These Russian boys, who have been fighting in the Kursk region, pose for a propaganda photograph in 1942. So many children were orphaned by the fighting on the Eastern Front that they were often adopted by army units. Pictures like this show that the Soviets were proud of their young fighters.

Children from Nazi-occupied territory in Eastern Europe and the Soviet Union were often imprisoned in camps and used as slave workers.

In this photograph on the right, taken in Berlin in 1945, Hitler is giving out medals to boys from the Hitler Youth who have been fighting the Russians.

Days from defeat, the Nazis thought nothing of sacrificing Germany's youth, even when there was no hope of victory. This is thought to be the last picture taken of Hitler before his death.

German girls were expected to help out by tending to wounded soldiers or air-raid casualties.

These British children shelter in a ditch as RAF fighter planes take on German bombers in the Battle of Britain. Their faces show a mixture of excitement and trepidation.

Many British children were evacuated from cities to the relative safety of the countryside. Those who didn't lose close relations often remember the war as an exciting adventure.

"Everyone has died.

Only Tanya remains."

12-year-old Tanya Savicheva records the annihilation of her family during the Leningrad siege in 1942. She survived another couple of years, dying in 1944, the year the siege ended.

This photograph has often been used to represent the inhumanity of the Nazis. It shows frightened Jewish children being rounded up with adults in the Warsaw Ghetto in 1943. They are all almost certainly bound for the gas chambers of Auschwitz or another Polish death camp.

These French children play on a knocked-out German half-track vehicle – a remnant of the fighting in Normandy, following the D-Day landings in the summer of 1944.

Their war was not as horrific as the one endured by Russian or Polish children, but they are still lucky to be alive. Around 20,000 French civilians caught up in the fighting in Normandy lost their lives.

A line of German refugees flees from the advancing Soviet Army. Along with emaciated horses are cattle and other farm animals.

Chapter 5

The end

Even as the War drew to its inevitable conclusion,
German and Japanese leaders were determined not to
give up. In Nazi Germany, anyone who dared to suggest
that the war could not be won could be punished by
execution. Japan's military rulers were also determined
to keep fighting. In the final year of the War, millions
more were to die – both soldiers and civilians – as Allied
attacks reduced Japanese and German cities to rubble.

British paratroopers,
during the attack
at Arnhem

Germany from the West

Those expecting a quick end to the War after the
Normandy Landings were to be disappointed:
Germany was far from finished. It took the Allies six
weeks to break out from their landing zones,
followed by fierce fighting in Normandy. Then,
finally, the Allies headed for Paris, which was
liberated on August 25, 1944.

A bridge too far

The Belgian cities of Brussels and Antwerp were
liberated on September 3 and 4, and a week later,
the Allies crossed into Germany. But here they
stopped. A pause was needed to rest and resupply.
   Montgomery suggested a daring plan: to use
parachute troops to seize three bridges in the
Netherlands, to open the way into Germany from
the North. They captured bridges at Eindhoven and
Nijmegan, but failed to hold the most important
one, Arnhem. Of the 10,000 men parachuted to
Arnhem, 8,000 were killed or captured.

The liberation of Paris

In August 1944, Hitler sent
orders to destroy Paris, but
the German commanding
officer, Major General
Choltitz, refused to obey.

As the Allies approached the
city, the French police, who
had been under German
control, went on strike.
Then Resistance groups
came out into the open.

As the Allies entered Paris,
they encountered sporadic
but stubborn resistance
from the Germans, but
there was mercifully little
bloodshed.

The Battle of the Bulge

While the Allies licked their wounds, the Germans launched a surprise attack in the Ardennes region of Belgium on December 16. Using powerful new tanks, and soldiers dressed in US uniforms, the Germans swept through Allied troops, spreading panic. It became known as the Battle of the Bulge, after the large hollow it made in the Allied line.

But, on December 23, overcast skies turned to blue, giving the Allies a chance to make use of their superior air power. The German assault ground to a halt, as Allied planes cut a swathe through their tanks with rockets and cannons.

Counting the losses

The battle was one of the bloodiest of the War in the West. The Americans lost 19,000 men, but the Germans fared far worse. Around 600 tanks and heavy guns were destroyed, and up to 100,000 men were killed or captured. Hitler would never be able to attack in such force again.

Germany destroys itself

The Allies entered Germany in force in March 1945. In many places the Nazis fought back with the same tactics they had used on the Eastern Front.

As they retreated, they destroyed power stations, hospitals, schools and bridges. Much of the industrial heartland of the Ruhr Valley was deliberately flooded. Even some German leaders raised concerns about this destruction of their own country.

German troops pass blazing Allied vehicles during their daring counterattack in December 1944.

Germany from the East

Lesser armies would have collapsed after the dual defeats of Stalingrad and Kursk. But the Germans were formidable foes. They had arguably the best trained and equipped army in the world, their young soldiers having spent their childhoods being indoctrinated in the Nazi youth organization, the Hitler Youth. Even in the face of defeat, they fought on with courage and determination.

But Soviet soldiers continued to drive Hitler's armies back to Germany, despite the fact that in every battle the Russians lost far more men. Soviet resources now completely outmatched the Germans, and their army was twice the size.

The Year of the Ten Victories

By the end of 1944, the Russians had all but driven the Germans from the Ukraine and Belorussia (now Belarus). Bulgaria, Romania, Hungary and the Baltic States followed and, finally, Poland. The Russians called it, 'The Year of the Ten Victories'.

Soviet soldiers, proudly displaying their combat medals, line up for a propaganda photograph on the German border.

German prisoners of war march through Moscow. After they passed, the streets were washed down in a gesture of contempt. They face a daunting future and few would return home.

The Warsaw Uprising

In July, 1944 as Soviet forces approached the German-occupied Polish capital, Warsaw, Moscow radio called on its citizens to rise up against the Germans. Within four days, a Polish underground 'Home Army' of 40,000 men and women had reclaimed much of the city. But the Germans held off the Soviets, and then turned on the Home Army. In brutal house-to-house fighting that lasted for 63 days, over 200,000 civilians are thought to have been killed.

Realizing that their struggle was lost, the Poles negotiated a surrender. They could all have been executed as partisans, but the 15,000 members of the Home Army who survived were marched off to prisoner of war camps.

During the Warsaw Uprising, Polish fighters wore white and red armbands to distinguish themselves as combatants.

Operation Bagration

Between June and August 1944, in one vast operation, codenamed *Bagration*, the Soviets destroyed German forces in central Russia. German losses were huge: 300,000 killed, 250,000 wounded and 150,000 captured.

The German front line was now to back where it had been at the start of 1941. German soldiers and civilians now faced an enemy determined to take revenge for the suffering and destruction the Nazis had caused.

81

Berlin falls

In February 1945, the Russians stood on the banks of the Oder river, an hour from the eastern outskirts of Berlin. They paused to build up their strength.

To the west, the British and US forces were also closing in on the capital, but it had been decided between them that the Soviets would occupy Berlin.

Many of the last defenders of Germany were old men or frightened teenage boys, like this one. They faced execution if they refused to fight.

Hitler's bunker

Hitler spent most of the last months of the War in his bunker beneath the streets of Berlin. More and more out-of-touch with reality, he directed non-existent armies and grew increasingly shrill in his denunciation of his people.

"Those that remain after the battle are those who are inferior; for the good will have fallen," he declared.

Showing no remorse for what the Germans had suffered in the War, he continued to blame the Jews for the conflict.

Thousands of Berliners fled west, leaving a city already damaged by bombing. As the Soviets invaded, a ragged army largely made up of tired veterans, old men and boys, was recruited to defend the city.

In the street-fighting that followed, Berlin suffered further devastation. Squads of Nazis would patrol the streets, executing any soldiers caught deserting their posts. Some of the more fanatical units fought in hand-to-hand combat against Soviet troops.

The last stand

Final losses are difficult to confirm, but 450,000 German soldiers may have died in the battle for Berlin, along with 125,000 civilians. On the Soviet side, 81,000 were killed and 280,000 wounded. For an army that had pushed the Germans back from Stalingrad and Moscow, it was still a very high price to pay for the battle that ended their War.

On April 30, with Soviet troops closing in on him, Hitler committed suicide in his underground bunker. On May 7, 1945, the German army surrendered and the War in Europe was over.

Hitler's end

After the double suicide of Hitler and his new wife, Eva Braun, Nazi officials doused their bodies in fuel and set them alight.

Soviet soldiers later found the bodies and buried them secretly. But they were dug up and burned again, and the ashes scattered in the Elbe river.

In one of the most famous pictures of the War, a Russian soldier risks his life to raise the Soviet flag on the German parliament, the *Reichstag*, in the middle of a devastated Berlin.

US Marines unload supplies on the island of Iwo Jima. US military strength made Japanese defeat inevitable.

Kamikaze

Since October, 1944, the Japanese had encouraged their more inexperienced pilots to crash their planes deliberately into US ships and bombers.

These pilots, known as *kamikaze* (meaning 'divine wind'), were especially successful at Okinawa. In a total of 800 attacks, 32 US ships were sunk and a further 368 damaged.

Aircraft carriers were prime targets. Suicide missions were also carried out by Japanese submarines, speedboats and manned missiles called *Ohka* (meaning 'cherry blossom'), which were launched from a larger aircraft.

Iwo Jima and Okinawa

As the war in Europe was grinding to a bloody end, the US Marines were still fighting the Japanese in the Pacific. But two major obstacles stood in their way: the islands of Iwo Jima and Okinawa. Both were considered Japanese territory, and Japan had not been invaded for 4,000 years.

The Iwo Jima campaign

The tiny, volcanic island of Iwo Jima was now home to 20,000 Japanese soldiers, who had constructed an ant's nest of fortresses and tunnels inside it. The Americans arrived with an invasion force of 800 ships and 300,000 men, including 100,000 Marines — soldiers trained for combat on both land and sea. The first wave landed unopposed.

But, as the beaches filled with men and equipment, Mount Suribachi, the hilltop on the southern tip, 'lit up like a Christmas tree' as the Japanese opened fire from their hidden bunkers. The counterattack had begun. It took a month for the world's greatest military power to destroy the Japanese garrison.

On to Okinawa

The long, narrow, inhabited island of Okinawa had been fortified with 100,000 Japanese troops. They too had created a dense network of tunnels and strongpoints to defend it. The US attack began on April 1, 1945, but it took 13 weeks of fighting, often in driving rain, to take the island. The mud and squalor of the battlefield was so awful that Okinawa was compared to the trenches of the First World War.

The next stop for America was mainland Japan – a task they looked on with increasing trepidation.

Fighting to the death

On Iwo Jima, the US lost 6,000 men, with a further 17,000 wounded. All but 216 Japanese soldiers fought to the death or commited suicide.

Taking Okinawa cost the Americans a further 5,500 dead and 51,000 wounded. Over 11,000 Japanese soldiers surrendered, but this was still only 10% of their total strength.

Tragically, an estimated 150,000 civilians were killed or commited suicide. They were influenced by Japanese propaganda that depicted US soldiers as barbarians who would rape, torture and kill them and their children.

The blast-torn landscape of Okinawa, shown here, reminded veteran US soldiers of the battlefields of the First World War.

A knockout blow

This view of Hiroshima was taken soon after the bomb had flattened the city. The 'T' shape made by the intersecting bridges on the right was used by the bomber crew as a drop point for their weapon.

In the 1930s, scientists had discovered that certain atoms contained tremendous energy which could be unleashed with devastating effect. During the War, a race began to develop an atomic bomb. The US plan, codenamed the *Manhattan Project* and directed by brilliant US physicist Robert Oppenheimer, cost two billion dollars and involved 600,000 employees. But it was so secret that even Vice President Harry Truman didn't know about it.

By the early summer of 1945, the US team had a bomb ready for testing. Its core of radioactive materials was about the size of an orange, but it had the destructive power of 20,000 tons of TNT, the most common explosive at the time. A trial firing in the New Mexico desert was a success. Hiroshima, an important Japanese port and weapons depot, was chosen as the first target.

Two devastated cities

On August 6, 1945, the B-29 bomber *Enola Gay* flew over Hiroshima, dropping the bomb on the city. The explosion killed 80,000 immediately, and much of the city was flattened. The damage was so great that survivors thought it was the end of the world. Within weeks, a further 80,000 had died from injuries and radiation sickness.

The Japanese government thought the reports so extraordinary they dismissed them as exaggerations. But, three days later, another B-29, *Bock's Car*, dropped a bomb over the city of Nagasaki. The same day, the Soviet Union invaded Japanese-held Manchuria, intending to go on to invade Japan itself. Deciding they couldn't risk another atomic bomb and a Soviet invasion, the Japanese agreed to surrender on August 15.

Japan surrenders

Japan signed a surrender on September 2, 1945, aboard USS *Missouri* in Tokyo Bay. It was six years and a day after the War had begun in Poland.

In a naked display of American power, the bay was filled with warships, and hundreds of planes flying overhead in formation. The reason for Japan's defeat could not have been clearer.

The world after the War

The War ended in a mixture of celebration and despair. There were street parties in the cities of the victorious nations. Survivors felt elation and guilt as they remembered lost friends. Now they faced an uncertain future.

Millions of people displaced by the fighting needed to be rehoused, cities had to be rebuilt and stable, democratic governments needed to be set up in place of the fallen dictators. Lessons had been learned from the disastrous treaty which had ended the First World War. But German and Japanese politicians and military leaders, and others who had collaborated with them, were tried and punished for war crimes.

The cost of war

At least 50 million people, civilian and military, died in the War. Some estimates of the number of deaths are even higher.

• Soviet Union: at least 20 million

• China: up to 20 million

• Germany: 5.5 million

• Japan: 3.6 million

• Britain and the British Empire: 490,000

• USA: 292,000

• Poland: over 6 million (including 3.5 million Jews) – one in six of the population

In an Allied camp for people displaced by the War, French photographer Henri Cartier-Bresson captures the moment a camp inmate recognizes a Nazi informer. She will be lucky to escape with her life.

Nuremberg trials

German war criminals were tried before an international court at Nuremberg. The worst offenders were hanged.

Dame Laura Knight's painting of the Nuremberg Trial (left) imagines accused Nazi politicians and military commanders surrounded by the devastation they brought to Europe.

Dividing Germany

Germany, and its capital Berlin, was divided into four zones of occupation. In 1949, two separate states were created: East and West Germany. In the East, Berlin remained divided between East and West, with a wall built in 1961.

For the next 40 years, the Soviets retained political control in East Germany. In 1989, the Berlin Wall was torn down, and Germany was re-unified soon after.

The legacy

To help rebuild Europe, the US government offered aid to all countries, regardless of which side they had been on. Help was also given to rebuild Japan.

Meanwhile, the War enabled the Soviet Union to control Eastern Europe. Along with the USA, it emerged as a new superpower, and the two became bitter rivals. For the next four decades, the threat of another global war, and even nuclear annihilation, loomed.

The Second World War was the most destructive event of modern times. It cast a shadow over the rest of the 20th century and its legacy is still with us today.

Joint British and American zone

BERLIN

British zone

Soviet zone

French zone

American zone

Timeline of the Second World War

Here are the major events in the story of the Second World War.

September 1939

Nazi Germany invades Poland. Britain and France declare war on Germany on September 3.

April 1940

Germany invades Western Europe. *Blitzkrieg* tactics win them stunning victories.

June 1940

France surrenders. Only Britain remains at war with Germany.

July 1940

The Battle of Britain begins. The Germans fail to defeat the RAF. In September, Hitler postpones his plan to invade Britain.

June 1941

Nazi Germany launches *Operation Barbarossa*, a massive invasion of the Soviet Union.

October 1941

German troops are stopped just before Moscow, in a battle which lasts until January 1942.

December 1941

Japanese aircraft attack the US base at Pearl Harbor. Germany declares war on USA too.

October 1941

32 Allied ships are sunk by German U-boats in one night, during the Battle of the Atlantic which lasts throughout the War.

September 1941 to January 1944

The siege of Leningrad

December 1941 to May 1942

Japan conquers much of the Eastern Pacific region, including Hong Kong, Singapore and the Philippines.

January 1942

At the Wannsee Conference near Berlin, Nazi chiefs plan the Final Solution: industrial-scale murder of millions of Jews.

May 1942

The Battle of Coral Sea halts Japan's southern expansion in the Pacific

June 1942

The Battle of Midway ends Japan's western expansion in the Pacific.

August 1942

The Battle of Stalingrad begins. It ends in February 1943 with a crushing defeat for German forces.

August 1942 to November 1943 — In the Pacific, US forces defeat Japanese troops from Guadalcanal to Tarawa.

October 1942 — The Battle of El Alamein ends German hopes of control of North Africa.

July to August 1943 — The greatest tank battle in history takes place at Kursk. On the Eastern Front, Nazi forces begin a long retreat.

July to August 1943 — Allies invade Sicily, then the Italian mainland.

September 1943 — Italy surrenders and German forces there become an occupying power.

October 1944 — The greatest sea battle in history takes place at Leyte Gulf. Japan loses 26 ships; USA 7.

August 1944 — Warsaw Uprising against the Germans. It ends in October.

August 1944 — Paris is liberated by US and French forces.

December 1944 — German troops counterattack at the Battle of the Bulge, but do not have the strength to make good their initial gains.

September 2, 1945 — Japan signs a surrender and the War in the East is over.

February 1945 — Dresden is destroyed by the RAF.

February 1945 — US Marines invade Iwo Jima.

August 1945 — US B-29 Superfortresses drop atomic bombs on Hiroshima and Nagasaki.

May to August 1944 — US forces conquer Pacific islands from Biak to the Marianas.

June 1944 — D-Day – the Allied invasion of Western Europe. 150,000 land on the first day.

April 1945 — The Battle of Berlin begins.

April 1945 — US Marines invade Okinawa.

May 8, 1945 — VE Day: Germany surrenders and the War in Europe is over.

April 30, 1945 — As Soviet soldiers capture Berlin, Hitler commits suicide.

Glossary

This glossary explains some of the words you may come across when reading about the Second World War. Words in *italics* have their own separate entries.

aircraft carrier A large, long-decked warship from which aircraft can take off and land at sea.

air raid An attack on a target, often a town or city, by bombs dropped from enemy planes.

Allies The nations that fought against the Axis. The main Allied powers were Britain and its *empire*, the Soviet Union, the United States and France.

appeasement The policy of permitting Germany's territorial expansion in the run-up to the Second World War, in the hope of avoiding conflict.

armaments The weapons and *munitions* used by a military force.

atomic bomb An explosive weapon that releases enormous energy by splitting elements such as uranium or plutonium.

auxiliary A person who works to support the armed forces, but who isn't directly engaged in combat.

Axis Collective term for the countries who opposed the *Allies*. This meant principally Germany, Italy and Japan, but also included Slovakia, Romania, Hungary, Croatia and Bulgaria

battalion A unit in the armed forces, comprising a large number of soldiers who are organized into several different groups.

battleship A large, armed and fortified warship.

Blitzkrieg A fast-moving attack, using tanks, motorized troops and aircraft, used to great effect by the German army at the beginning of the War. (The word means 'lightning war' in German.)

bunker An underground defensive position or protective chamber.

civil war A war in which armies from the same country fight each other.

civilian Anyone who is not a member of the armed forces.

colony A geographical area under the political control of another country.

Commonwealth The association of countries which were formerly members of the British *empire*.

communism A political system in which the state controls the wealth and industry of a country on behalf of the people. People who follow this system are called Communists.

convoy ships Merchant ships that travel in a group, with warships to protect them from attack.

concentration camp A guarded prison camp where *civilians* and political prisoners are held during wartime, usually under harsh conditions.

death camp A *concentration camp* where the captives are deliberately killed or worked to death.

dictator A ruler who imposes his rule by force.

economy The financial system of a country.

empire A group of countries or territories under the control of another country.

evacuate To send troops or *civilians* away from a threatened area, for safety. During the Second World War, many *civilians* were evacuated from cities to rural areas.

fanaticism Extreme devotion, beyond the point of reasoning or logic.

fascism A system of government usually run by a *dictator*, often characterized by extreme *nationalism*, in which opposition is suppressed by terror and censorship.

front line The boundary along which opposing armies face each other.

garrison A military base or fortification.

ghetto A densely populated, enclosed district of a city, set up by the *Nazis* to keep the Jewish population cordoned off from the rest of the population.

Great Depression The period of worldwide unemployment and poverty, which began after the Wall Street Crash of 1929.

Holocaust The term given to the Nazis' systematic slaughter on a massive scale of European Jews and other groups during the Second World War.

incendiary bomb A bomb that is designed to burst into flames on impact.

kamikaze A Japanese word meaning 'divine wind', which referred to a plane loaded with explosives to be piloted in a suicide attack.

League of Nations A diplomatic organization set up after the First World War, made up of countries pledging to settle disputes without resorting to war.

Luftwaffe The name of the German air force before and during the War.

machine gun A gun that can fire bullets very quickly without needing to be reloaded.

Maginot Line A line of underground fortifications, 140km (87 miles) long, built by the French along their border with Germany during the 1930s. Designed to prevent a German invasion.

Marine A member of the US Marine Corps, an American body of sea-going troops.

morale The collective spirit or confidence of a group of people.

munitions Ammunition, such as bullets, bombs and *shells*.

nationalism The belief that nations benefit from acting independently, rather than in cooperation with other nations. Extreme nationalism results in the belief that one nation is superior to all others.

Nazi Party The *nationalist*, violent political party led by Adolf Hitler, known in full as the 'National Socialist German Workers' Party'.

occupy To seize and take control of an area.

officer Usually a senior member of the armed forces.

partisan A member of a group of independent, armed *resistance fighters*.

patriotism Loving one's country and being prepared to fight for it.

prisoner of war A soldier captured and held by the opposing side during wartime.

propaganda Information that is systematically spread to promote or damage a political cause.

RAF The Royal Air Force – the British air force. Pilots came from Britain and the *Commonwealth* and also from *occupied* nations in Europe.

radar A system that uses radio waves to detect and determine the distance of airborne objects.

radiation Energy given off by atoms. With some materials, such as uranium and plutonium, this radiation can be harmful.

refugee A person who is forced to leave their homeland, usually fleeing dangers such as war, famine or persecution.

reparations Payments made by Germany to several Allied nations after its defeat in the First World War, justified as being compensation for causing the War.

resistance fighters A member of secret organizations that fought to overthrow the enemy forces *occupying* their country, especially in France.

revolution The overthrowing of a leader or government by the people, usually by violent struggle.

sabotage To damage or destroy property and utilities in order to hinder an enemy's progress.

Scorched Earth A military tactic that involves destroying anything that might be useful to the enemy, while advancing through or withdrawing from an area.

shell A hollow missile containing explosives.

sniper A rifleman or woman who takes shots at enemy soldiers from a concealed position.

SS An elite unit of the German armed forces that served originally as Hitler's personal guard and as a special security force in Germany and the occupied countries. SS stands for the German word *Schutzstaffel*, which means 'protection squad'.

stalemate A situation where neither side can win, and no further action can usefully be taken.

submarine A ship which can travel underwater for long periods.

torpedo A self-propelled, explosive device which travels through water and can be launched from a plane or ship.

treaty An agreement between two or more countries.

U-boat A German *submarine*. The name comes from *Unterseeboot*, which means 'undersea boat' in German.

Index

Acknowledgements

Every effort has been made to trace and acknowledge ownership of copyright. If any rights have been omitted, the publishers offer to rectify this in any future editions following notification. The publishers are grateful to the following individuals and organizations for their permission to reproduce material on the following pages: t=top, m=middle, b=bottom; r=right, l=left

cover: main tank image © Hulton-Deutsch Collection / CORBIS; SE Asia map © Bettmann / CORBIS 1 © The Art Archive / Alamy; **2-3** © RIA Novosti; **4-5** © Science and Society Picture Library / Getty Images; **6-7** © Estate of Norman Wilkinson / National Maritime Museum, Greenwich; **10-11** © Mary Evans Picture Library / Alamy; **13** © Henry Guttmann / Hulton Archive / Getty Images; **16** © Fotosearch / Getty Images; **14** © Photos 12 / Alamy; **15** Cartoon by Clifford Kennedy Berryman © CORBIS; **20** Mainichi Newspaper / www.aflo.com; **21** © Mary Evans / INTERFOTO; **19 tr, tl** United States Holocaust Memorial Museum*; **22-23** © The Print Collector / Alamy; **24** © CORBIS; **28-29** © CORBIS; **30** © Imperial War Museum (MH_006547); **31** © CORBIS; **32-33** © Pictorial Press Ltd / Alamy; **34** © Keystone / Hulton Archive / Getty Images; **35** © RIA Novosti; **36-37** © Bettmann / CORBIS; **38** © Paul Popper /Popperfoto / Getty Images; **40-41** © akg-images / ullstein bild; **43** © Bettmann / CORBIS; **44** © Mansell / Time & Life Pictures / Getty Images; **45** © Hulton-Deutsch Collection / CORBIS; **48-49** © Roger Viollet / Getty Images; **50** © CORBIS; **51** © The Art Archive / Culver Pictures; **52** © Gamma-Keystone / Getty Images; **53 t** © Bettmann / CORBIS; **53 br** © K.J. Historical / CORBIS; **54** © Yad Vashem Archive; **56 tl** © CORBIS; **56 br** © Photo Scala, Florence / BPK, Bildagentur fuer Kunst, Kultur und Gesichte, Berlin; **57 tl** © Imperial War Museum (IWM_PST_003645); **57 mr** © De Agostini / SuperStock; **57 bl** Poster by A. Kokorekin © Photo by Laski Diffusion / Getty Images; **58-59** © Dargis / US Army / National Archives / Time Life Pictures / Getty Images; **60** National Museum of Naval Aviation; **61** National History and Heritage Command; **62-63** Battle of El Alamein by William Longstaff, 1942, courtesy of the Council of the National Army Museum, London; **64** © akg-images / Alamy; **65** © akg / De Agostini Picture Library; **66-67** © RIA Novosti; **68-69** © Associated Press; **70** © INTERFOTO / Alamy; **71** © Bettmann / CORBIS; **72** © Associated Press; **73** © Time & Life Pictures / Getty Images; **74 b** © Heinrich Hoffmann / Timepix / Timelife Pictures / Getty Images; **74 t** © RIA Novosti; **75 t** © Black Star / CORBIS; **75 m** © Imagno / Hulton Archive / Getty Images; **75 B** © Mirrorpix; **76-77** © Hulton-Deutsch Collection / CORBIS; **78** © CORBIS; **79** © CORBIS; **80** © RIA Novosti; **81** © INTERFOTO / Alamy; **82** © CORBIS; **83** © Yevgeny Khaldei / CORBIS; **84** © George Eastman House / Getty Images; **85** © W. Eugene Smith / Time Life Pictures / Getty Images; **86-87** © Hiroshima Peace Memorial Museum, Photo by Shigeo Hayashi; **88** © Henri Cartier-Bresson / Magnum Photos; **89** © Imperial War Museum (IWM ART LD 5798)

* The views or opinions expressed in this book, and the context in which the images are used, do not necessarily reflect the views or policy of, nor imply approval or endorsement by, the United States Holocaust Memorial Museum.

Picture research by Ruth King

Digital manipulation by John Russell